Where the Lotus Blooms

Neha Radhika Chand

◆ FriesenPress

One Printers Way
Altona, MB R0G 0B0
Canada

www.friesenpress.com

Copyright © 2023 by Neha Radhika Chand
First Edition — 2023

All rights reserved.

No part of this publication may be reproduced in any form, or by any means, electronic or mechanical, including photocopying, recording, or any information browsing, storage, or retrieval system, without permission in writing from FriesenPress.

ISBN
978-1-03-916931-9 (Hardcover)
978-1-03-916930-2 (Paperback)
978-1-03-916932-6 (eBook)

1. POETRY, SUBJECTS & THEMES, WOMEN AUTHORS

Distributed to the trade by The Ingram Book Company

Where the Lotus Blooms

Land Acknowledgement

As a first generation Canadian, this land is so much more than home. It is not only the land we speak of when we think of landscapes, borders, and development. For many, this land represents freedom, opportunity, and resilience.

In the 90s my parents immigrated to Canada from Fiji Islands. They may not have known much about Canada, yet they arrived with degrees that were not recognized and steadfast faith in the land.

For me this land is the mother that opened her arms to my parents and many immigrant families when they spent years sacrificing themselves for better health care, income and generational security.

When people look at me and my brown skin, and ask me where I am from, I want it to always boil down to the fact that I was born here. So, to be a part of Truth & Reconciliation, and to take a moment to acknowledge the land, is my chance to appreciate her, that has given me so much without asking for anything in return, a debt I cannot repay.

Before I am Indian and before I am Fijian, I am Canadian. Before I am Canadian, I am an ally of my buried brothers and sisters under unmarked graves. If I am made from the air, soil and ether of any land on Earth, it is this land. This soil has fed, nourished, and protected me. It has educated me and healed me.

I appreciate doing this land acknowledgment because I am also a daughter of Treaty 7 territory.

So, in the spirit of reconciliation, I would like to acknowledge the traditional territories and oral practices of the Blackfoot Nations, which includes the Siksika, the Piikani, and the Kainai. I also acknowledge the Tsuut'ina and Stoney Nakoda First Nations, the Métis Nation, and all people who make their homes in the Treaty 7 region of Southern Alberta.

Table of Contents

Svaha 1

Fire

Fire is the epitome of purity. One cannot taint or tarnish it. She can be a gentle flame, flickering in an oil lamp. She can be rampage, violent and destructive. She is the source of life and the inevitable torch to a pyre. The themes within the poems within this chapter cover the dualities within us and around us. This again emphasizes the importance of both the masculine and feminine energies of creation. These dualities are the source and maintenance of our world.

Queen	2
Death of *Him*	*4*
Be Ablaze	6
Distorted	8
Just Us	10
Until Then	12
Waiting	14
Averted	18
Grief	20
Fear in Your Eyes	22
Bearing Our Burden	24
Guru	26
Performance	30
The Difference	32
No one knows	34

According to the Hindu Vedas, Svaha is the goddess of sacrifices. She is the consort of Agni, the God of fire. Her name is taken during all fire prayers to sanctify the ceremony.

Prithvi

Earth

The Earth is the heart and chest of a mother. She who absorbs the sins of her children and the violence upon her soil. The mother who swallows her tears to shower her children with nourishment. She will tremble only to tear herself apart, while her blood swells and storms. This chapter explores the depths of the Earth's creations and our interconnectedness to the endurance and resilience she teaches us of, through her forests and flowers. We look to her to learn how to carry our burdens with grace and humility.

Mother	38
Where the Lotus Blooms	40
Tamed Wildflowers	42
I Am Wild	44
Despite you	46
Clenched Teeth	48
Silent Auction	52
Glimpses	54
Honest Deceit	56
Sewn Lips	58
Inner Children	60
Daughters	62
Shedding	64
Sacrifice	66
Call it Even	68
Selfish Murder	70
Illusions	72
The universe within *her*	*74*
Diamonds	76
Pink Hibiscus	78
Girmityas	82
Soiled Soil	84
Hollow Trees	86
Gratitude	88

Prithvi derived from the Sanskrit word for Earth. The word is also used for the Hindu Goddess of Earth, Prithvi Mata.

Bhagirathi

Water

Water is the mind and senses, uncontrollable and impossible to grasp. Water is a life source and in constant change and flow. Water can be soft and elegant yet can smoothen the roughest of rocks. The beauty between us and water is that we are like the rivers of the world. We are rushing and pouring into one another, yet are destined for unity. We are diverse are rivers of spirit in the ocean that is the universe. This chapter highlights our interconnected identity, the cycles we experience and the constant change and fluidity of life.

The Love of God	92
Oneness	94
Kingdoms	96
Fault	98
Whitewashed	100
Homogenous	102
Marionette	104
Lucid	106
Fog	108
Translucent	110
Eye of the Storm	112
Waves	114
Pain of Past Tense	116
Thankful	118
Karmic Cycle	120
Breaking the Cycle	122

Bhagirathi is a Himalayan River, which according to Hinduism, is the source of the Ganges.

Chapter 1

Svaha

Queen

No matter how hard you try to scar and tarnish the skin of
 a lioness
No matter how hard you try to tame her
No matter how hard you try to muffle her roars
she remains the queen of the jungle
she remains the chosen chariot for the divine feminine
so, taint her
spit on her
throw dust into her face
bite and attack
but when the dust settles
the lioness remains the same
no matter how surrounded she is.

Death of *Him*

My ego seeks validation
I go looking for loyalty,
I want to know that you know me.
I want your devotion
My ego fears its death and nurtures life
While death is our constant
and life is unfaithful
The death of my ego is as inevitable as death
yet he lives in his web of illusions
but maybe the day he is killed
I will truly begin to live.

Be Ablaze

Under the flickering light
We have prayed
We have learned
We have cried

Each flickering light starving for life
Writhes in his death to adorn your eyes with light
Eventually each blaze is exhausted
and is cremated into the air

In its life and death
we fixate on our suffering
rather than the flickering light
that warms us when we pray
illuminates as we learn
and dries the tears of our cries

Distorted

For how long will we pluck and pick at each sacred text
destabilize someone's foundation
to uphold our own
How long will we preach, pick and choose
the verses that justify your actions
your spoken words, my idols, your literature, my scripture
Why is oppression *religious* when you do it?
Why is feminism *culture* when we do it?

Just Us

We are still those baby sisters
With sunlight in our faces,
wind blowing in our hair
We are out waiting
In the dewy warm grass
Waiting for you to come home and play.

Will you come back to play?

Is it your embrace in the wind?
Is it your warmth in the sunlight?
The gentle raindrops?
Are those your colours in the sunset?

Because it was us
who raced with the wind
Hid in the shadows from the sun
Laughed with the thunder in the rain
Until the day was finally done

We are still those baby sisters
Waiting with lamps in our hands
It's smoke in our faces
The hurricane in our hair

Waiting for you to say
We can play again, you are coming home.

Until Then

I hope I look beautiful to you
When my eyes lose its hazel
Every strand on me ablaze
When my rage settles on the pyre
When my voice no longer plays

The instruments that beat within me
Will stop making music for you
And when my pulsing body goes numb
I hope that's when I look beautiful to you

Waiting

We were waiting.
To wear blue.
To decorate your mandap[1].
To play in turmeric.
To pick the colours of the flowers.

We were going to witness.
You take your vows of life.
Around a sacred fire.

But a brother lowered his sister's palanquin off his shoulder that day.
Before she could lift a mala[2] made in your name.

Instead, our brothers lifted you onto their shoulders.
Us sisters, lowered a mala in your name.

We were dreaming of blue skies and warmth.
We never saw the storm that came.
We still had your procession.
None of it was the same.

---

1 Mandap: A decorated platform made for religious ceremonies.
2 Mala: Flower Garland

Waiting

Alas we wore your blue.
built your mandap and picked colours for flowers.
But instead, we anointed you in oil.
and we prayed around a pyre.

We learned to walk and run together.
We played until sleep filled our eyes.
You will always be the hope in my prayers.
Like the relief in one's painful cries.

I tied sacred threads around your wrist.
as brothers and sisters do.
I prayed for your protection.
I know you did it too.

We will protect your reputation.
We will honor your legacy.
I will always be proud of you.
I hope you are proud of me.

Ill set aside a rakhi[3] each year.
For when we meet again.
The Gods were simply generous.
When they let us keep you from heaven.

---

3   Rakhi: A sacred thread given during the Indian festival of *Raksha Bandhan* as an amulet of protection and respect.

Averted

Sometimes it's hard to look in the mirror
It is hard to look at your own palms and not see the gentle parts
we choose to see the rough edges, to glorify our
    demanding work
we count our wrinkles and grey hairs because I have it worse
    than you

It's so easy to preach
It's so much harder to practice
to find my own flaws and work on them
To sit with it, to let my thoughts sit alone with me
So, I keep talking my talk, so I can drown out my demons
It is hard to look in the mirror

Grief

This must be the grief we only heard about
From a distance
From a glance

Now in the eye of a storm
I can't even hear it
The thunder and waves crashing
I only feel it
Deep in my heart

So deep I know its there
I feel it even when i forget

The ache that is left
The scars etched on me
I don't tend to these wounds
I leave them open
I don't have the strength to heal them
I would rather feel them.

Fear in Your Eyes

I dread becoming a mother
I could probably do it
I could do it well
I would nurture and architect
No more moulding and shaping
But I am afraid

My motherhood might make me un-justify everything I told my inner child
I told her there were reasons
I shaped and moulded so many excuses

I am so worried that holding my own children might unveil.
There was never a good reason.
Nothing could be justified.
I am not afraid for myself.

Bearing Our Burden

It is such a misconception
That you can share my grief
That would mean you would take from me
Make mine less
Make mine light

Yet my burden is just as heavy and now you have some more.

Grief is more like a sizzling flame
It chews at the wick of our life
We simply ignite each other
Only creating a more violent blaze

It singes the wicks of our life
Then we share our scars and burns
But we can never share our grief.

Guru

It can feel like black velvet
Weighing on your shoulders
Adorning you, in its simplicity
In its richness of nothing
Its void
Yet its depth is unfathomable ignorance
The danger is in mistaking the darkness as empty
It is full of the meaningless, the idle and the abandoned
It is asphalt
It's when you don't know you're in it
That's when you need to know
Like quicksand
Don't struggle
Trust me

Guru

Let me save you from the tar
Enrich you in pure silks
Hold my hand and let me enlighten you
I won't open your shackles
I won't pull you through
I will hold the quivering flame and you walk to me
I'll hold your hand if you falter
We will steady the light of wisdom
Don't fear the shadows
Embrace them, bring them with you

Let us illuminate the world
With humility in our eyes
Prayers on our tongues
The abstract in our hearts
And a rhythm in our souls
So, when I'm gone
When the paper in me crumbles
And the ink in my veins dries
You will take my light
And awaken others
Save the world, my child

Performance

You taught me pride,
I became idyllic
wife, daughter, goddess
each time
you destroyed me
I gathered myself

but I lost that seed, those roots—they died,
the fire within me . . . of idealism

so now I perform the roles
I am not them anymore
I re-enact them

I am not perfect
You think I am perfect
You think I am perfect because I am a reflection
A reflection of your beauty, of your soul, your eyes
A reflection of who I used to be

I want to be just like you
Your voice is like the thunder
It trembles my heart, it's raging
but would never strike

Your love is the showers that pour
I want to be the rainbow that comes from a single drop of your essence
I want to show the world that I am you, your creation

The Difference

You speak louder
You pray with your face
You stand the tallest
You know the words
You sing the hymns
I also speak, I pray, I stand, I know, I sing, but the difference is
When the bells stop ringing
When the chants come to a silence
You leave the same as you came
        head high
I leave the same as I came
        lowered eyes.

No one knows

The world may not know me
You're right, they don't know me.

But,
I am not alive to please the senses of fellow humans.
I am not on Earth for praise of fallen angels.

I am on Earth to be in sync with the divine
Because she knows me
My God knows me
She knows each corner of my heart
Along with the depths of my fear

I am grateful the world doesn't know me.
That I am not entangled in it's maya.
I am one with the world. I am the world.
The world that doesn't know me.

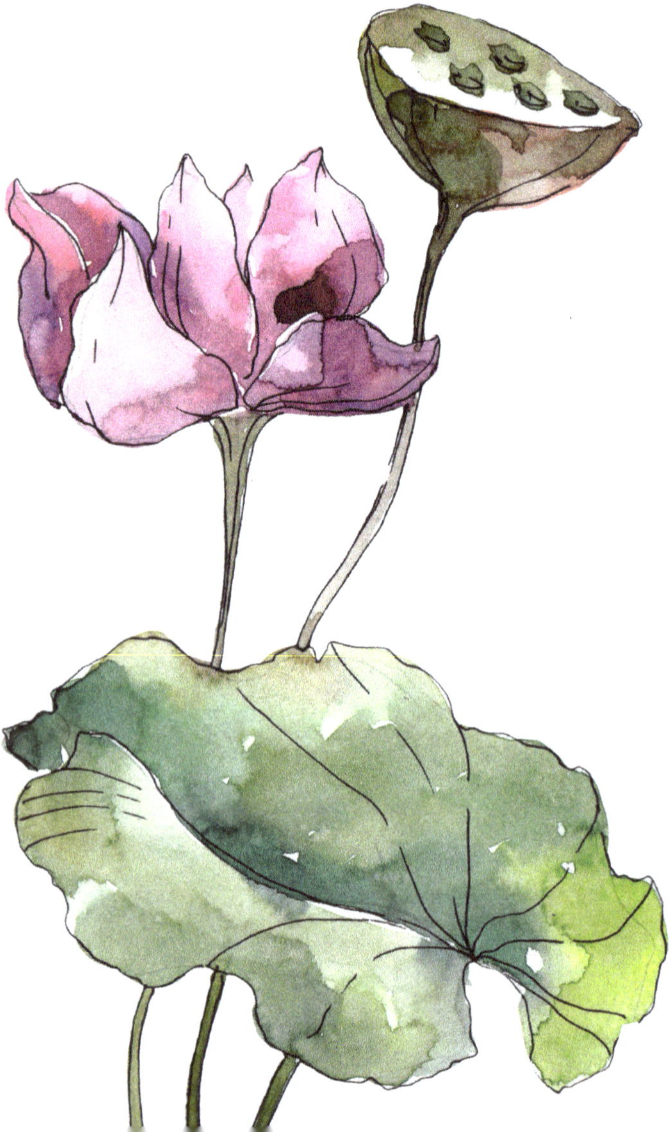

Chapter 2

Prithvi

Mother

When I write,
She wonders why
I don't print her on my pages
Why she's not enough to be written

When I invoke my purest emotions
I am still not able to create from her

What could I create for my creator herself
The paper and ink are you and I
I am embedded into you
my worth is from what you've made of me

If I could, I would carve you into the stones of mountains
I would whisper your essence into waters
describe your vibrancy to flowers
enlighten my footsteps with your legacy

If I could, I would immortalize you
So, the earth remembers my goddess

But I will find you in every life
Like a muse finds her artist
A verse their poet
A prophet their god

So, when you wonder when I write
Why I cannot write you
It is because I cannot confine my worship
Words cannot embrace
A mother
The written is not enough

Where the Lotus Blooms

carrying the world on its petals
stemming the universe from its roots

in impure waters, the lotus blooms

the tarnished and soiled
rooted in mud
blossoms without a stain
it blooms exquisite

remember to be the lotus

circumstances may be soiled
grow, ascend
untainted and resilient

Tamed Wildflowers

I thought when God planted his garden,
He let his flowers grow wild
He let petals blow in the wind
He let nectar sweep through the air
So, when did humans start plucking flowers?
When did we decide we own them?

Now as gardeners, we plant our seeds,
Watch them grow,
Water and feed, with the expectation of fruit
If my child bears no fruit
It should look at all the trees that do

But my child has sweet flowers
More royal than the next
Yet you put a stick through her roots to make sure she stands tall
You shove a trellis to her neck to make sure she grows how
   you want

So, my hair doesn't blow in the wind anymore
My fragrance doesn't carry in the air
I only face the sun when I am told
And grow how the gardener says.

I Am Wild

You keep learning and unlearning as your ravelled history
   becomes undone.

You look me in my eyes,
you tell me not to use the word *wild*

You looked at us and told us the *wild* was primitive
you told us we are *savage* animals
You open your mouth and snatch my words
because I speak until you're uncomfortable.

I am a wild, outspoken animal
don't scrape my tongue with your words
then seize my jaw to see
if the words bleed out to your fitting

I am an animal
To me, animals are the universe
our protectors and creators
I worship animals
you made them inferior

So, when you look into my eyes, I hope you see the animal
   in me
When you look at my curly mane, I hope you see the wilderness
I hope you see that you are only battling yourself

I have always been who I am,
You keep learning and unlearning as your ravelled history
   becomes undone.

Despite you

You thought you never broke me
Your words, your hands
It shattered me like a goddess sculpted in clay
Day by day

You tell me I am fearless because I never broke
You said if I broke, I was useless . . . a disgrace to a reputation
    without a name . . . an insult to a world without a god
That if I broke, I was weak

I broke
You broke me
I am not weak because I broke

I am strong because I gathered each shattered piece
I built myself up with every piece you tore off
You stepped on fragments while I was picking myself up
Keep them to remember me by

Because now I won't break.
I am not made from your blood anymore

What defines me is who I've become after I recreated my
    entire being

After I revived myself
I am my only inhale and my only exhale
My heart only beats for me

I hope you break, too
When your legs tremble to get up
When you're looking up at me
I'll lift you up
I'll let you grow
And you'll see the strength it takes to be defeated
The strength it takes to break.

Clenched Teeth

I learned to bite my tongue
I hold it down, so you don't suffer
I fuel your ego and light the fire in your eyes
because my silence becomes your passion
my silence gives you strength
so, you put your words in your books
your policies
your religions
your rights

you think my silence is my ignorance
my futility, my fragility
my silence is your blessing
because it keeps you running the world
my silence hums women, it hums justice, it hushes our power

we speak to each other through our eyes
we acknowledge how we raise you
how we feed you
cultivate you

Clenched Teeth

so, we let you speak, as if we didn't
you can feel us radiate our strength
like body heat, our powers pulse from us
but we bite our tongues
so, you can run your world

if we opened our mouths,
if sound came out
if we unclenched our teeth, our fists and minds
our voice would infiltrate your veins
it would fill every son's heart
our voice would turn to dust your ego
your birth, your being

you would lose every battle, every war
because you would know you're wrong . . .
because you don't run the world
our silence does.

Silent Auction

I am seated at the tallest seat
amidst the best of the best
sunlight on my face
illuminating the eyes of everyone

A crowd watches, I am acclaimed
my anklets shimmer
I've sat here for so long

The older I get
the veils are uncovered
The watchers make claims
the anklets are shackles
I am in the limelight
Going once, going twice.

Glimpses

We pull our sleeves down to our wrists
and tug our collars higher

We pull our shirts at our waists
and lower our gaze in the streets

We are never openly told, "it's not your wrists, shoulders or hips, my child"
It is the gaze of those who have shrouded their women in fear
Who have come to taint the daughters of others

They think their eyes innocently caress
They don't know it is daggers to our souls

Until we can truly see innocence in their eyes
Daughters will continue to pull on our sleeves, tug at our collars and pull our shirts past our waists.

Honest Deceit

I see a little girl
long black tresses
run through the streets in a playful dance
she asks each person she passes
to show her their palms
"Where did you put it?"
"Do you, have it?"

Tie your hair
walk slower
gaze lower

"Then will you give it back?"
"Show me your hands please!"

"I heard that they have it,
my name, my reputation, my worth, in their fists,
I want it back."

How can I explain to this woman
who has been fed this lie since birth
that they don't have it
They just make her think they do
so, she will dance to their tunes
and seek her worth in everyone else, but herself.

Sewn Lips

It starts when we are very little
When our smiles reach our eyes
And the sparkle of both is like stars bursting of fire
That's when, stealthily, with a needle and thread, our lips are sewn.

Not violently.
But with a thread labelled *elegant, feminine, obedient*

The older we get, stitches are added
Maybe because the pain grows, too?
Eventually our cries are just muffles
Inside our minds and inside our chests
And they have the audacity to ask, *What's wrong?*
As they guide my hand to paint a smile over the seam.

Inner Children

Every once in a while, I hear a sobbing so deep within my heart,
shrieks so loud that I stop in my path
the cries consume me and vibrate off my body
they are outside me now . . .
they are behind me

I turn to see a forest of me
some 5, some 15, some 25, some yesterday
each one has a cry, yearning for an embrace
I walk past each one and whisper, "You are enough—
   you were and always will be"
each muffled tear dries, as each child's thirst for validation
   is quenched

I go back all the time to see them,
to tell them I love them.

One day I will venture deeper into the forest and find
   my foremothers
I know their longing for healing runs deep in my blood
I hope to tell them, too, words that they never heard
"You are enough—you were and always will be"

Daughters

As soon as you hold her, it becomes inevitable
That you carry her without her being yours
You become hers
And her ignorance keeps her from the truth
That one day she will leave

She will carry what you give her
The light and fire it took to create the passion
In her eyes

With her knowledge, she will illuminate generations
With her fire, she could disintegrate.

Shedding

I will wrap my arms around your feet
And watch each finger slip off
As I cave
As I forgive myself for running out of chances

I let you go so you don't stay
And once the last fingertip caresses the dust of where you stood
You walk away with the satisfaction of thinking you left

You'll never know how I let you go
It's because I let you leave

It's only when I wanted to
That I let you walk away.

Sacrifice

She was once a small sunflower
In new bloom
Her gaze would follow her creators
Like the sunflower to the sun

Her creators gave her breath
Sometimes heavy showers
She feared their thunder
But bathed in their warmth

As she grew, she glowed with the youth of a rose
With royal colours radiating through her

Yet she was ignorant of the fact that
Just as the roses are
She was also meant to be severed
To fragrant a different home

When she leaves,
Will the trees weep for her?
Will the garden's flowers not ask where she went?
They will go, too, and some will stay
This is the sacrifice of the flowers.

Call it Even

I had no remorse pulling the petals off those rose stems
I was giving my brother to the Earth in return.

Selfish Murder

They love me, they love me not,
round and round you always go
With each pluck, we diminish the breath of the flower to tell
   ourselves we are loved
We pick and tear apart the flower
and wallow in the misery of our tattered hopes as we land on
   loves me not
Then we toss the carcass of luck

We turn and walk away alone
But the garden catches the petals to whisper to her that they
   loved her,
and bury her in their arms.

Illusions

The instruments you play were once sacred
to be touched by the hands of the pure
knowledge only given to learned men
they never even let us learn
we were lucky if we got to listen

now you taint them with your plumes of smoke
and have muddied my culture with your bowls of water
you have taken what was once knowledge that belonged to
   the worthy
and have declared yourselves the unworthy sages that
will now tell our generations how we pray
in plumes of smoke
intoxicated in the mystical illusion of God
in the grasp of the devil

The universe within *her*

She might not be your heir
She may not rule kingdoms
but like the earth, she bears your violence
like the rain, she quenches your thirst

She won't carry your name
But she will carry your sins

She will hide them in her veil
And sacrifice them in her name

She will heal your ego
as she disguises her wounds
She will ignite your passions
while you succumb to yours

She will raise warriors
feed nations
birth daughters
who will carry her story
her name
her heir

Diamonds

Let me burn
Let me feel the earth on my chest
Let burdens wound my back
Let my shoulders crumble,
I'll dust them off
Don't stop your words, the eyes or your hands
From trying to grasp me, crumble me, break me
I'll slip through your fingers while you look down at filth
I'll dust them off
I'll decorate you
But first, let me burn
Let me feel the earth on my chest

Pink Hibiscus

I pressed her into the pages of my book
the book with hymns of home
the oceans and hills
the sacred dust of villages
and the hurricanes of faith

she is pink and I call her hibiscus
she's my home and my heaven
she gives me comfort

I remember
the modest laughter of my mother
the look of protection and worry from my father
but the sweat 'n' tears were for our tomorrow

so, all of us pressed our flowers
we bowed to the earth that gave us birth
to live our lives in the arms of another mother

she might have wept
but we left
to become less exotic

we left in different directions
instead of the shade of palm trees
the evergreens catch the snow
now it's cold rivers
where a warm ocean breeze used to blow

when the snowflakes hit the glass
a tear shatters
like a tropical raindrop on the veranda

it toughens my courage yet
softens the heart
but I do it for tomorrow

Pink Hibiscus

so, I place a maple leaf
in the hand of my child
and tell him it's a symbol of his mother
that is our today and tomorrow

the red may have transferred
from one flag to another

but I honour the soil of both
the one who made me a daughter
the one who made me a mother

If I could go back, I will
To take the earth and place her on my forehead
Like a son to his mother's feet

I will tell her how far I've come
how I miss her fragrance
how the world's fruit can't compare to hers

until then, I tell her in my heart
that I am always her child

I'll immortalize her to my children
and tell her stories like songs

Even though here I enjoy every season
With lights and colours of every nation

even when
I look to the mountain peaks of snow
and the chinook of every colour

nothing is as radiant
as the hibiscus pressed
within the pages of my heart.

Girmityas

In another life I must have dreamed
To work shoulder to shoulder with the white man
To speak their ways and live their life

My ancestors must have blessed these wishes

Reborn, I now live among them
I have replaced silks and gold with denim and stones
I have attained my karmic desires

Yet there is a void in my heart
For a land I have never seen
For a home I have never had

I must be cursed to yearn to return
To the heaven we abandoned for paradise.

Soiled Soil

You came with hands full of soil
From the womb of where you had blossomed
You brought it and grasped it so tightly
That your clench carries blood and tears

You sit on the abundance of a different land
but you have held the fragrance of home for so long you fear
   that this air may soil it

As you grow old, you ask us to open our palms
as you pour these sands into our hands
some sift between our fingers as you pour—lost
some mix with the soil we have been moulded with—enhanced

We cannot spoil them
so, we grasp
and carry on
with hands full of soil

Hollow Trees

The ancient trees that were able to speak and were revered
the ones we call the wise old oaks
The roots have withered as the earth has grown old
yet the wise ones use it as their cloaks.
these trees don't impart wisdom anymore
they are hollow but stand so tall
we all go and bow our heads at their feet
and praise their old wise wisdom
but the essence, the spirit, of the wisdom is gone
false preachers stand tall in their shadows.

Gratitude

I promise you; I know.

I recognize
I appreciate
I value

My generation is grateful
We are empowered
We are blessed
We are, because you did

We may not feel indebted
We may not carry legacies
We may not fulfill footsteps

Who really does?
Who decides?
Who dies, knowing they did?

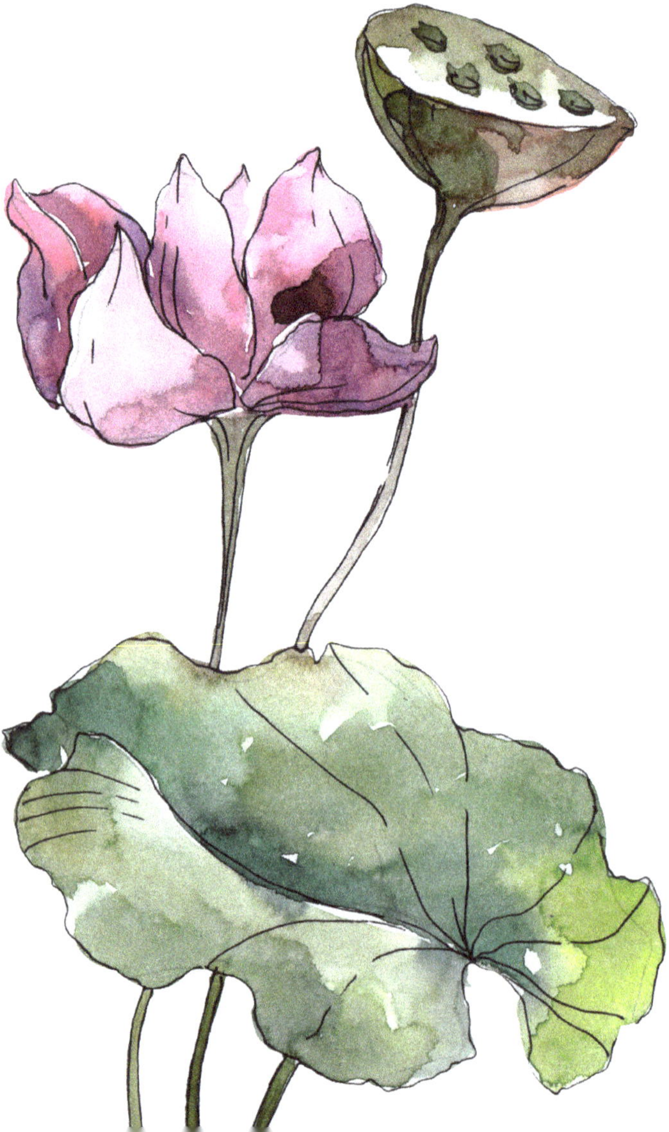

Chapter 3

Bhagirathi

The Love of God

I wish I loved you
while you adore me
while your eyes caress me
your touch refines my beauty
I wish what I felt was the love that you feel

what I feel is beyond expression
beyond a word that is bound by language
beyond communication, words 'n' letters
it's something that maybe the universe could encompass

it's the high within a praise
breathlessness at the highest peak
humility in the ego

it's a worship
a devotion

the blush of an embrace
the lowered gaze of a bride
the fear of death and the relief of survival
I wish I loved you
what I feel for you is the gravity that binds the earth and sun
your love gives me the moon's luminosity
it's not within me, but reflects you

I feel the rush of a hurricane and the trembling of thunder
the storms that are not confined by nature, the love not
   confined by words

yet I'll say, "I love you"
I'll use the word "love" to tell you
I am the word, and you are my language
I am bound to you.

Oneness

Take me to the forests that have died to write our scriptures
Take me under the Banyan trees that have heard our seers speak
They are our witnesses
Ask them if they know the difference

Take me to a tree that I can shear
with each sliver of paper
I want to write my Gita, my Gurbani, my Quran and my Bible
Before I leave with my gods in my hands
I will ask their maker
"What is the difference between these pages?"
and she will know none
all are brothers created from one.

Kingdoms

I don't want to tear your kingdom apart
I just want back what is ours

Give us back our dignity that you took with our jewels
Give us back the gold and respect
Give us back our women and spices
You took and created your empire
Once we have what is ours
Your castles will be left hollow
You will hear the chants of my ancestors
That died for freedom from your kingdom

Fault

Each milestone could always be better
I could have done better
There was always someone who did better
So, every brick I built myself with had cracks
   of dissatisfaction.
And they wonder why I became a broken woman.

Whitewashed

They drink their culture
and are intoxicated in worship
when we grow
we don't find peace
we find no clarity in their haze
Then they say we are the lost ones
Lost touch with the orange, green and white painted across my face?
Is it the blue, red and white that pours off my tongue?
Or have these colours merely smeared when you try to wash the red and white from me?

Homogenous

As the waterfalls ebb and bend
I wonder are we the fall, the milk or the silence below?
The fall are those who enjoy their high and crash
Adventurous and Courageous
Are we the milk that is churned beneath this freedom?
Churned and mixed into a homogenous identity
Am I the silence that follows? Do I flow back into stillness?
Should I quench the thirst of adventure and seek each creek in the earth
Or am I destined to lose myself in the ocean?

Marionette

Each limb hangs off the threads of expectation
to you, it's how I sing and dance for spectators
You put on a show like a puppeteer
as I hang off the nooses you've tied to my body.

Lucid

There are so many grey spaces in the world, nothing can explain
No science
No religion

Places in the world, in the mind and in the soul

Hazy
Dreamy
Sultry
A place both familiar and dangerous
The place between waking and sleeping

The time between seconds
I want to live there
In the peace of that blur before sunlight
The pause before the needle tick
Let me live in the trance where no one goes, and where no one will find me

Fog

The language I speak
Although it is volume for me
It is silence for the rest

I write, then erase
I type, then backspace
The words that are not present are the ones I need you to see
The visor of my words should guide

Why can't I write that poetry anymore?
I sit down

I'll call myself the earth to paint the picture
Of the two worlds that fuel my creation

Translucent

If I poured your words into my hands
Like ink
And painted my reflection with you
The opaque reflection
If I swiped your likes and comments off each screen
And painted my face with your validation
The only image I would see in the mirror would be just that—
 an image . . . not my reflection.

Let us remember the beauty of translucency
Not everyone deserved to see you, to know you
They shall see what we wish
There are depths to my soul only I can venture
But we can dance in the mists of our spirits.

Eye of the Storm

It struck
An eerie silence
The shock wave that shook the earth
Went through our bodies
The deafening silence in our shrieks

The evil eye must not wander from far
That we were shaken from our pedestals so quickly
Falling onto the earth

We were at a standstill
A shock
Helpless and Paralyzed

Walking with the storm is the true pain
Because I haven't even grasped what has happened
But now we are crawling our way out of darkness.

Waves

It comes and goes
The laughter, the smiles
No matter how hard I laugh, it will never be as loud
No matter how bright my smile, it could be wider
No matter how much joy comes around
It will never be as much

As what would have been
If you were here.

Pain of Past Tense

Each day felt like the curves and waves in the w
That has replaced the i
In every sentence
From is to was

Thankful

I wish I could go back and hold little me
hold her tight in my arms
wipe tears in sadness
pat her pat in rejoice
hand on her shoulder for strength
hand in hand in fear.

Though, there is never going back,
I hold myself now
I tell myself,
"Go easy on me".
"Thank you, for me".
"Even if everyone leaves, be there for me".
I know I will thank myself one day
for making myself feel loved.

Karmic Cycle

There is such a beauty
In knowing that each moment and each breath of this life
I deserve it completely.

Every cry, I owed tears to someone.
Every laugh, someone repaid their debt.
In moments of anger, we have settled scores

We have all interconnected
intertwined
in such a complex way

with connections so deep
that we come back to fill wounds
left from another life

Breaking the Cycle

Before we put a pause to our journey

Let us leave behind our emotions
Let us only take our healing with us
Let us forgive the people that came to mind
Let us be humbled by the ego that may have risen

Let our ego ignite into the fire of these pages
Let our wounds bleed into the earth of my lines
Let the roars of water wash away our cries

Let us leave better than we came
We will meet again
Where the Lotus Blooms

Printed in the USA
CPSIA information can be obtained
at www.ICGtesting.com
JSHW061238021023
49435JS00001B/2

9 781039 169319